A Blimp Can Pass

by Clint Campo
illustrated by Hector Borlasca

Practice Decodable 22

McGraw Hill Education

Bothell, WA • Chicago, IL • Columbus, OH • New York, NY

MHEonline.com

Send all inquiries to:
McGraw-Hill Education
8787 Orion Place
Columbus, OH 43240

ISBN: 978-0-02-145623-9
MHID: 0-02-145623-2

Printed in the United States of America.

7 8 9 CTM 23

A class can pass. Scott naps.

A blimp can pass blocks.

A blimp can miss traffic.

What? The blimp has a hiss!

The blimp can cross and land fast.

Did Scott miss a call? It was the boss!